For Davy
—B.F.

For Ken
—S.A.

Design by Florence Ma.
Typeset in Chaparral Pro and Calligraphic 421 BT.
The illustrations in this book were rendered in gouache.

Text copyright © 2009 by Betsy Franco.
Illustrations copyright © 2009 by Shino Arihara.
All rights reserved. Published by Scholastic Inc., 557 Broadway, New York, NY 10012,
by arrangement with Tricycle Press.
Printed in the U.S.A.

ISBN-13: 978-0-545-27448-7
ISBN-10: 0-545-27448-6

1 2 3 4 5 6 7 8 9 10   08   19 18 17 16 15 14 13 12 11 10

Zero Is the Leaves on the Tree

by BETSY FRANCO

illustrations by SHINO ARIHARA

SCHOLASTIC INC.
New York Toronto London Auckland
Sydney New Delhi Hong Kong

Zero is...

the shape of an egg.

Zero is a number.

Zero is...

the balls in the bin at recess time.

0 balls

Zero is...

the leaves on the bare,

brown arms of the oak tree.

0 leaves

Zero is...

the ducks on the pond when
the air says winter is coming.

0 ducks

Zero is...

the sound of snowflakes
             landing on your mitten.

0 sounds

Zero is...

the sleds on the hillside
when the snow turns to slush.

0 sleds

Zero is...

the kites in the

sky once the wind stops blowing.

0 kites

Zero is...

the blossoms in the garden
just before the buds open.

0 blossoms

0 bikes

Zero is...

the bikes in the bike rack
on the last day of school.

Zero is...

the ripples in the pool

before the first swimmer jumps in.

0 ripples

Zero is...

the footprints on the beach

when the waves come in and in and in.

0 footprints

Zero is...

the sound of stars filling the night.